HAL•LEONARD
ESSENTIAL SONGS

PIANO VOCAL GUITAR

The 1990s

P9-AFO-417

ISBN 0-634-09105-0

HAL•LEONARD®
CORPORATION

7777 W. BLUEMOUND RD. P.O. BOX 13819 MILWAUKEE, WI 53213

CONTENTS

AC-CENT-TCHU-ATE THE POSITIVE

Lyric by JOHNNY MERCER
Music by HAROLD ARLEN

ADIÓS

English Words by EDDIE WOODS
Spanish Translation and Music by ENRIC MADRIGUERA

ALL OR NOTHING AT ALL

Words by JACK LAWRENCE
Music by ARTHUR ALTMAN

ANGEL EYES

Words by EARL BRENT
Music by MATT DENNIS

ANNIVERSARY SONG

from the Columbia Picture THE JOLSON STORY

By AL JOLSON
and SAUL CHAPLIN

ANYTHING YOU CAN DO

from the Stage Production ANNIE GET YOUR GUN

Words and Music by
IRVING BERLIN

I'm su-pe-ri-or, you're in-fe-ri-or.

I'm the big at-trac-tion, you're the small. _ I'm the ma-jor one,

you're the mi-nor one, I can beat you shoot-in', that's not all. ___

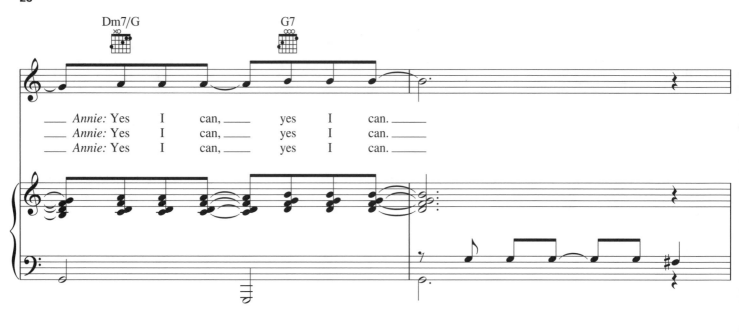

Annie: Yes I can, yes I can.
Annie: Yes I can, yes I can.
Annie: Yes I can, yes I can.

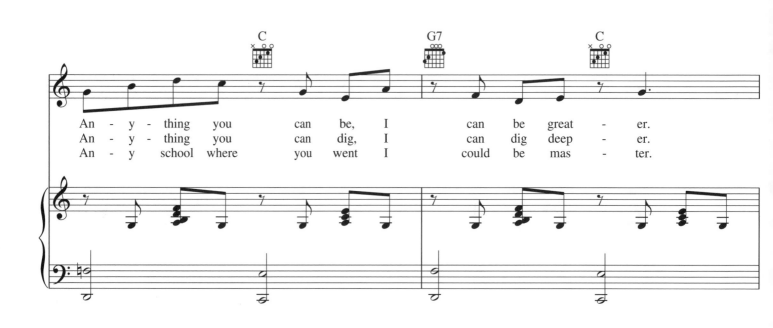

An - y - thing you can be, I can be great - er.
An - y - thing you can dig, I can dig deep - er.
An - y school where you went I could be mas - ter.

Soon - er or lat - er, I'm great - er than you. _Frank:_ No you're not.
I can dig an - y - thing deep - er than you. _Frank:_ Thir - ty feet.
I could be mas - ter much fast - er than you. _Frank:_ Can you spell.

BE CAREFUL, IT'S MY HEART

from HOLIDAY INN

Words and Music by
IRVING BERLIN

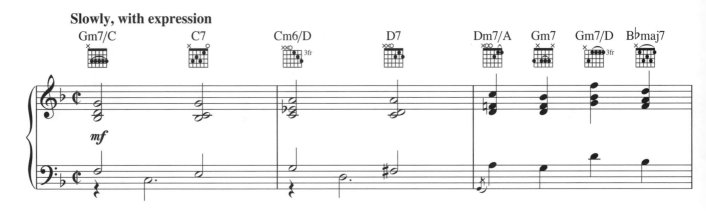

Slowly, with expression

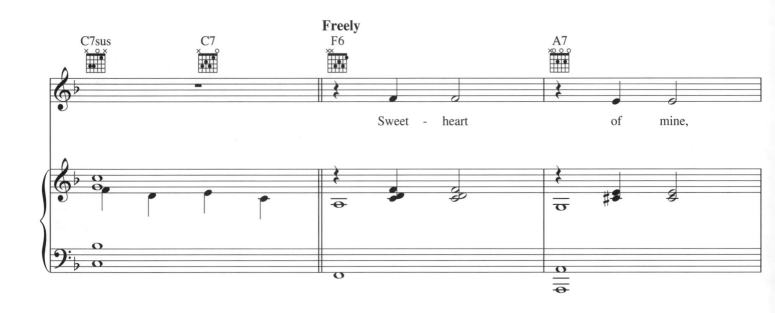

Freely

Sweet - heart of mine,

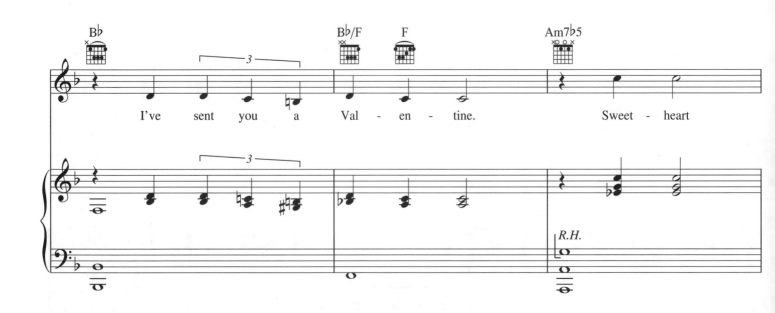

I've sent you a Val - en - tine. Sweet - heart

BEAT ME DADDY, EIGHT TO THE BAR

Words and Music by DON RAYE,
HUGHIE PRINCE and ELEANOR SHEEHY

BEWITCHED
from PAL JOEY

Words by LORENZ HART
Music by RICHARD RODGERS

He's a fool and don't I know it, But a fool can have his charms;

I'm in love and don't I show it, Like a babe in arms.

Love's the same old sad sen-sa-tion, Late-ly I've not slept a wink,

BOOGIE WOOGIE BUGLE BOY

from BUCK PRIVATES

Words and Music by DON RAYE
and HUGHIE PRINCE

Medium Boogie Woogie

He was a fa-mous trum-pet man from out Chi-ca-go way, ___ he had a "boo-gie" style that no one else could play. ___ He was the top man of his craft, ___

but then his num - ber came up, ___ and he was

gone with the draft. ___ He's in the ar - my now, a - blow - in'

re - veil - le, he's the boo - gie woo - gie bu - gle boy of Com - pa - ny B. ___ They

made him blow a bu - gle for his Un - cle Sam, ___ It
puts the boys to sleep with "boo - gie" ev - 'ry night, ___ And

BUTTONS AND BOWS

from The Paramount Picture THE PALEFACE

Words and Music by JAY LIVINGSTON
and RAY EVANS

CANDY

Words and Music by ALEX KRAMER,
JOAN WHITNEY and MACK DAVID

CHI-BABA CHI-BABA
(My Bambino Go to Sleep)

Words and Music by MACK DAVID,
AL HOFFMAN and JERRY LIVINGSTON

Tempo I

ba - ba, chi - ba - ba, chi - wa - wa. En - ja - la - wa, cook - a - la goom - ba. Chi -

ba - ba, chi - ba - ba, chi - wa - wa. My bam - bi - no, go to sleep. Chi -

ba - ba, chi - ba - ba, chi - wa - wa. My bam - bi - no, go__ to sleep.__ Chi -

ba - ba, chi - ba - ba, chi - wa - wa. My bam - bi - no, go to__ sleep.

COME RAIN OR COME SHINE
from ST. LOUIS WOMAN

Words by JOHNNY MERCER
Music by HAROLD ARLEN

CRAZY HE CALLS ME

Words and Music by BOB RUSSELL
and CARL SIGMAN

COMME CI, COMME ÇA

English Lyric by JOAN WHITNEY and ALEX KRAMER
French Lyric by PIERRE DUDAN
Music by BRUNO COQUATRIX

CRUISING DOWN THE RIVER

Words and Music by
EILY BEADELL and NELL TOLLERTON

DADDY'S LITTLE GIRL

Words and Music by
BOBBY BURKE and HORACE GERLACH

DAY BY DAY

Theme from the Paramount Television Series DAY BY DAY

Words and Music by SAMMY CAHN,
AXEL STORDAHL and PAUL WESTON

DEARLY BELOVED

from YOU WERE NEVER LOVELIER

Music by JEROME KERN
Words by JOHNNY MERCER

DOLORES

from the Paramount Picture LAS VEGAS NIGHTS

Words by FRANK LOESSER
Music by LOUIS ALTER

It was a sun-ny lit-tle, fun-ny lit-tle bor-der town _____ where on a moon-lit night I rode. _____ And all the lo-cal guys were vo-cal-iz-ing

DON'T GET AROUND MUCH ANYMORE

from SOPHISTICATED LADY

Words and Music by DUKE ELLINGTON
and BOB RUSSELL

A DREAM IS A WISH YOUR HEART MAKES

from Walt Disney's CINDERELLA

Words and Music by MACK DAVID,
AL HOFFMAN and JERRY LIVINGSTON

A DREAMER'S HOLIDAY

Words by KIM GANNON
Music by MABEL WAYNE

Ev - 'ry day for break-fast there's a dish of scram-bled stars, and for lunch-eon you'll be munch-in'

rain - bow can - dy bars. You'll be liv-in' a la mode on Ju-pi-ter or Mars

on a dream-er's hol - i - day. ___ Make it a long ___ va-

ca - tion; Time there is plen - ty of.

THE DUMMY SONG

Words and Music by LEW BROWN,
BILLY ROSE and RAY HENDERSON

EASY DOES IT

Words and Music by SY OLIVER
and JIMMY YOUNG

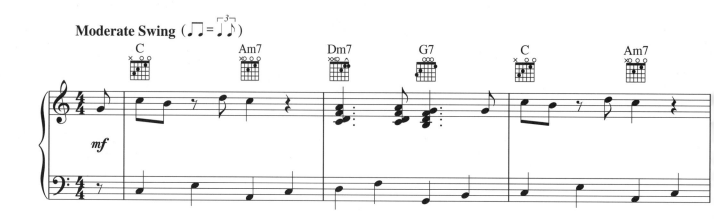

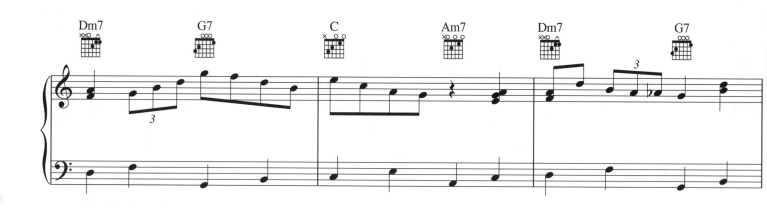

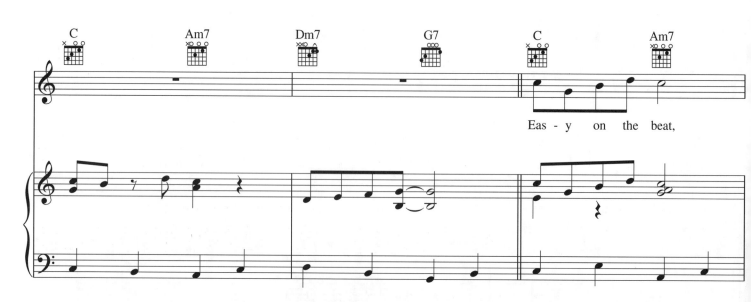

Eas - y on the beat,

FEUDIN' AND FIGHTIN'

Words by AL DUBIN and BURTON LANE
Music by BURTON LANE

ENJOY YOURSELF
(It's Later Than You Think)

Lyric by HERB MAGIDSON
Music by CARL SIGMAN

EVERYTHING HAPPENS TO ME

Words by TOM ADAIR
Music by MATT DENNIS

Black cats creep a-cross my path un-til I'm al-most mad, I must have 'roused the dev-il's wrath 'cause all my luck is bad. I make a date for golf and you can bet your life it rains, I

(I Love You)
FOR SENTIMENTAL REASONS

Words by DEEK WATSON
Music by WILLIAM BEST

love you _____ for sen-ti-men-tal rea-sons. _____

_____ I hope you do be-lieve me; _____ I'll give you my

GOD BLESS' THE CHILD

Words and Music by ARTHUR HERZOG JR.
and BILLIE HOLIDAY

THE FRIM FRAM SAUCE

Words and Music by JOE RICARDEL
and REDD EVANS

HAUNTED HEART

from INSIDE U.S.A.

Word by HOWARD DIETZ
Music by ARTHUR SCHWARTZ

HAVE I TOLD YOU LATELY THAT I LOVE YOU

Words and Music by
SCOTT WISEMAN

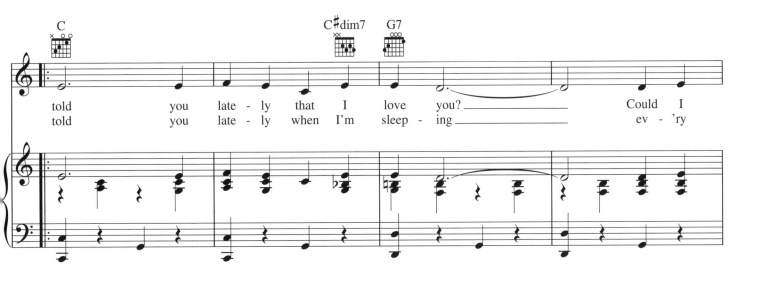

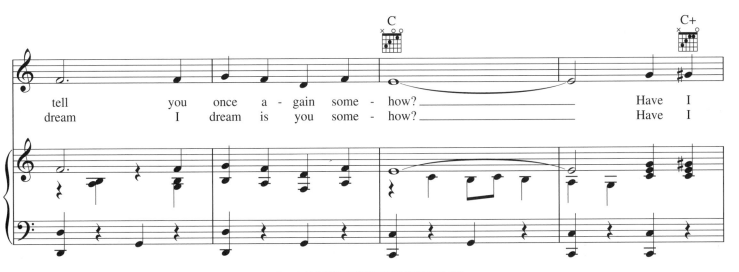

HEY! BA-BA-RE-BOP

Words and Music by LIONEL HAMPTON
and CURLEY HAMMER

HOW ARE THINGS IN GLOCCA MORRA
from FINIAN'S RAINBOW

Words by E.Y. HARBURG
Music by BURTON LANE

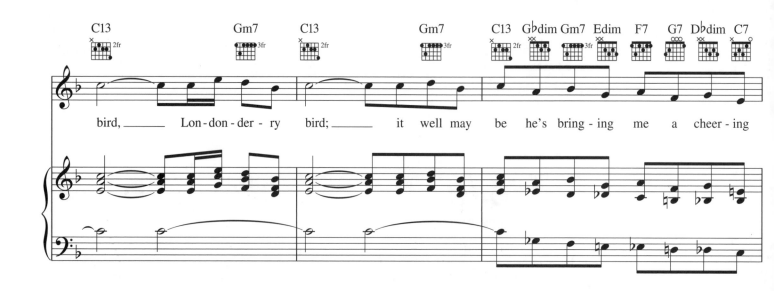

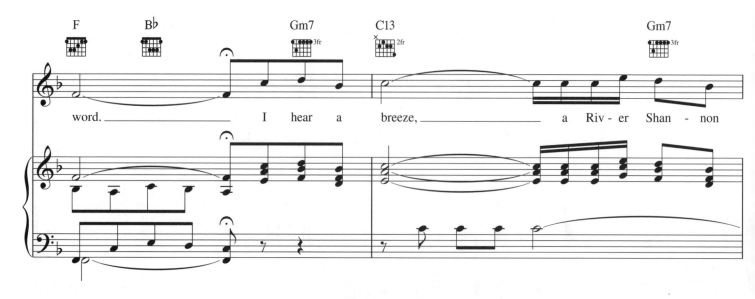

THE HUCKLEBUCK

Lyrics by ROY ALFRED
Music by ANDY GIBSON

Slow Blues tempo

I GOT THE SUN IN THE MORNING

from the Stage Production ANNIE GET YOUR GUN

Words and Music by
IRVING BERLIN

I COULD WRITE A BOOK
from PAL JOEY

Words by LORENZ HART
Music by RICHARD RODGERS

I DON'T WANT TO WALK WITHOUT YOU

from the Paramount Picture SWEATER GIRL

Words by FRANK LOESSER
Music by JULE STYNE

All our friends _ keep knock-ing at the door. They've asked me out _ a hun-dred times or more, but all I say _ is: "Leave me in the gloom," and here I stay _ with-in my lone-ly room. 'Cause,

I GOT IT BAD AND THAT AIN'T GOOD

Words by PAUL FRANCIS WEBSTER
Music by DUKE ELLINGTON

I GUESS I'LL HANG MY TEARS OUT TO DRY

from GLAD TO SEE YOU

Words by SAMMY CAHN
Music by JULE STYNE

I LOVE YOU

from MEXICAN HAYRIDE

Words and Music by COLE PORTER

I LOVE YOU SO MUCH IT HURTS ME

Words and Music by
FLOYD TILLMAN

I love you so much it hurts me.

Dar - ling, that's why I'm so blue.

I'm so a - fraid to go to

I WISH I DIDN'T LOVE YOU SO

from the Paramount Picture THE PERILS OF PAULINE

Words and Music by FRANK LOESSER

I REMEMBER YOU

from the Paramount Picture THE FLEET'S IN

Words by JOHNNY MERCER
Music by VICTOR SCHERTZINGER

I SAID MY PAJAMAS
(And Put On My Pray'rs)

Words and Music by
EDDIE POLA and GEORGE WYLE

I'LL REMEMBER APRIL

Words and Music by PAT JOHNSON,
DON RAYE, and GENE DePAUL

I'M A LONELY LITTLE PETUNIA
(In an Onion Patch)

Words by MAURIE HARTMANN and BILLY FABER
Music by MAURIE HARTMANN and JOHNNY KAMANO

I'M BEGINNING TO SEE THE LIGHT

featured in SOPHISTICATED LADIES

Words and Music by DON GEORGE, JOHNNY HODGES
DUKE ELLINGTON and HARRY JAMES

now when you turn the lamp down low___ I'm Be - gin - ning To See The Light____

Used to ram - ble thru the park ___ Shad - ow box - ing in the dark ___

Then you came and caused a spark,__ That's a four a - larm fire__ now_____ I

nev - er made love by lan - tern shine,__ I nev - er saw rain - bows in my wine,__ But

now that your lips are burn - ing mine,__ I'm Be - gin - ning To See The Light____ I _____

8vb

I'M OLD FASHIONED

from YOU WERE NEVER LOVELIER

Words by JOHNNY MERCER
Music by JEROME KERN

IN LOVE IN VAIN

Words by LEO ROBIN
Music by JEROME KERN

IS YOU IS, OR IS YOU AIN'T

(Ma' Baby)

from FOLLOW THE BOYS

Words and Music by BILLY AUSTIN
and LOUIS JORDAN

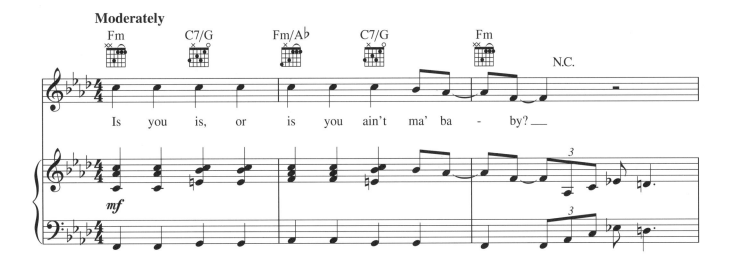

Is you is, or is you ain't ma' ba - by? ___

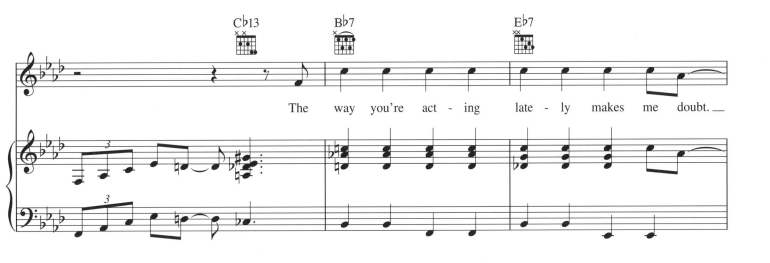

The way you're act - ing late - ly makes me doubt. ___

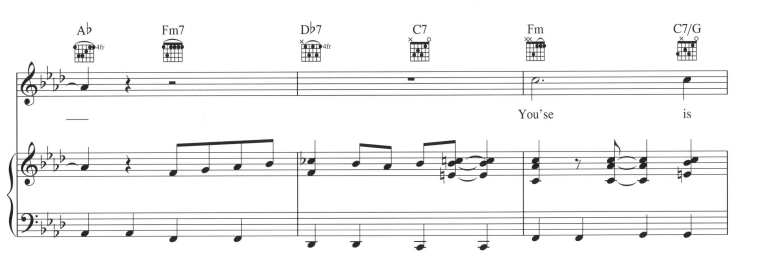

___ You'se is

IT COULD HAPPEN TO YOU

from the Paramount Picture AND THE ANGELS SING

Words by JOHNNY BURKE
Music by JAMES VAN HEUSEN

Do you be - lieve in charms and spells, in mys - tic words and mag - ic wands and wish - ing wells? Don't look so wise, don't

IT MIGHT AS WELL BE SPRING

from STATE FAIR

Lyrics by OSCAR HAMMERSTEIN II
Music by RICHARD RODGERS

Moderately

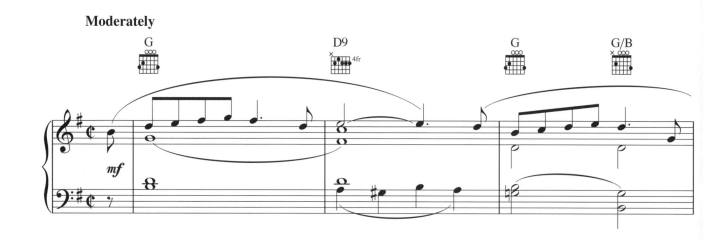

The things I used to like I don't like an-y-more. I

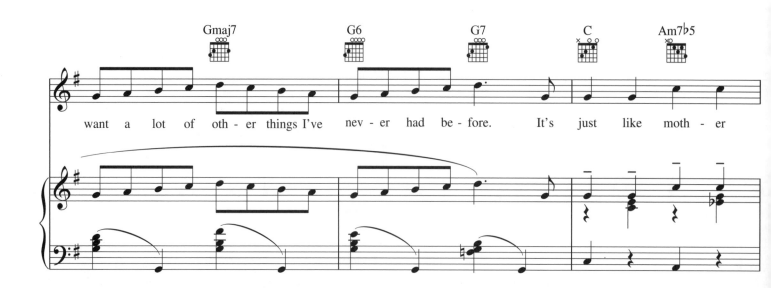

want a lot of oth-er things I've nev-er had be-fore. It's just like moth-er

IT ONLY HAPPENS WHEN I DANCE WITH YOU

from the Motion Picture Irving Berlin's EASTER PARADE

Words and Music by IRVING BERLIN

It on-ly hap-pens when I dance with you,

that trip to heav-en 'till the dance is through.

With no one else do the heav-ens seem

IT'S A GRAND NIGHT FOR SINGING

from STATE FAIR

Lyrics by OSCAR HAMMERSTEIN II
Music by RICHARD RODGERS

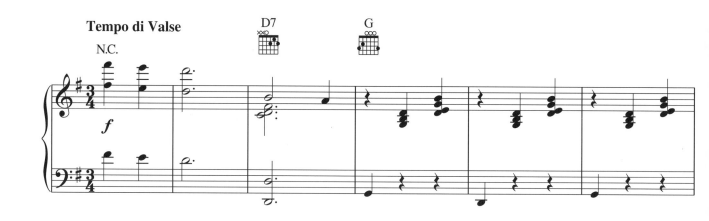

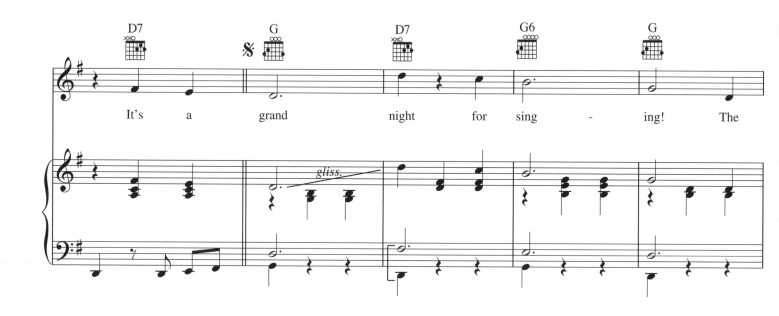

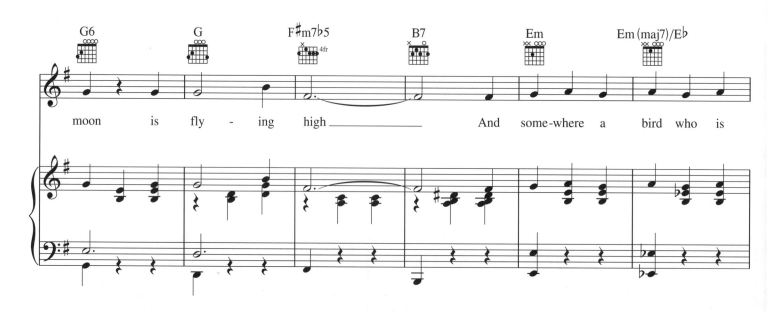

C7
G6/D
Am7
3fr
love.
Fall - ing,
fall -
gliss.
D7
G
C6
G
Fine
ing in love.
Interlude
N.C.
G
May - be it's more than the
mf
D9
4fr
D+
Gmaj7
moon,
May - be it's more than the birds.

IT'S A PITY TO SAY GOODNIGHT

Words and Music by
BILLY REID

Moderately, with a relaxed beat

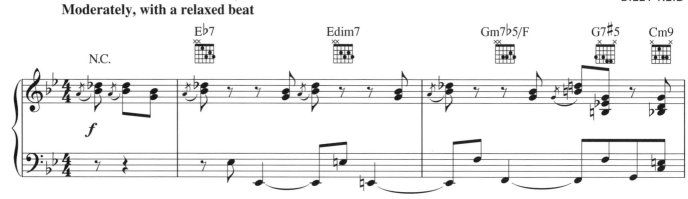

What a shame the

night is end - ing, cross my heart I'm not pre - tend - ing,

JUST A LITTLE LOVIN'
(Will Go a Long Way)

Words and Music by
ZEKE CLEMENTS and EDDY ARNOLD

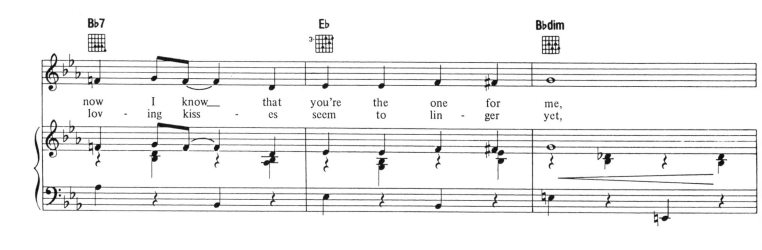

now I know___ that you're the one for me,
lov - ing kiss - es seem to lin - ger yet,

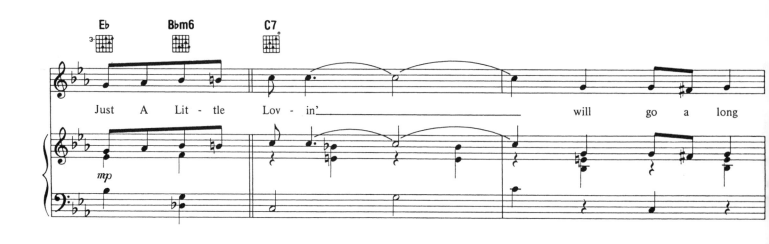

Come on back, and you will plain - ly see:___
I'll for - give but please, don't you for - get:___

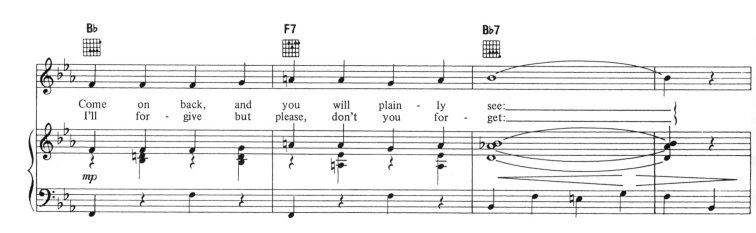

Just A Lit - tle Lov - in'___ will go a long

way,___ And you will make me hap - py___

JAVA JIVE

Words and Music by MILTON DRAKE
and BEN OAKLAND

JINGLE JANGLE JINGLE
(I Got Spurs)
from the Paramount Picture THE FOREST RANGERS

Words by FRANK LOESSER
Music by JOSEPH J. LILLEY

JUNE IS BUSTIN' OUT ALL OVER
from CAROUSEL

Lyrics by OSCAR HAMMERSTEIN II
Music by RICHARD RODGERS

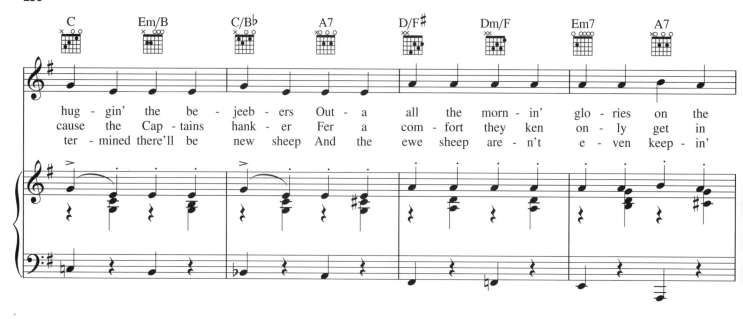

hug - gin' the be - jeeb - ers Out - a all the morn - in' glo - ries on the
cause the Cap - tains hank - er Fer a com - fort they ken on - ly get in
ter - mined there'll be new sheep And the ewe sheep are - n't e - ven keep - in'

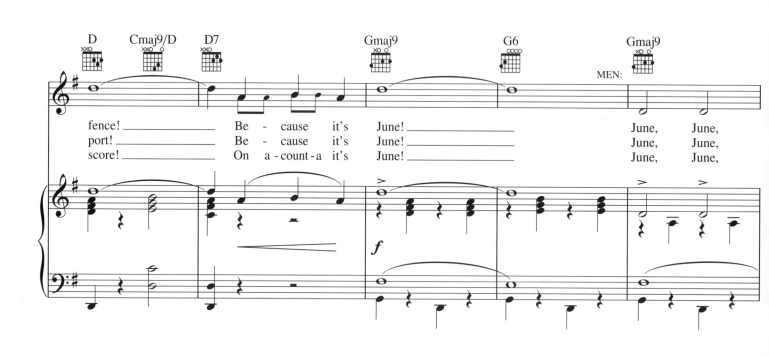

fence! _____ Be - cause it's June! _____ June, June,
port! _____ Be - cause it's June! _____ June, June,
score! _____ On a - count - a it's June! _____ June, June,

MEN:

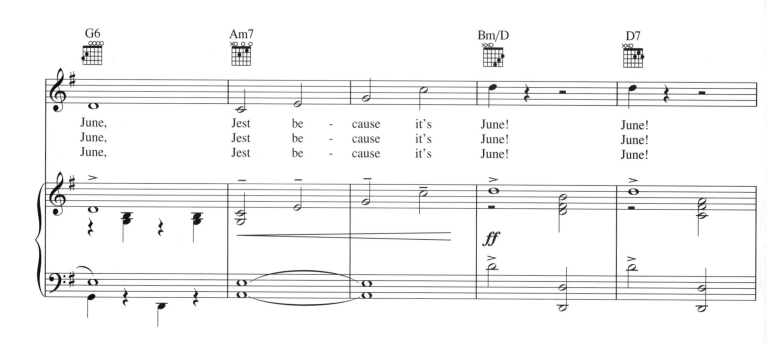

June, Jest be - cause it's June! June!
June, Jest be - cause it's June! June!
June, Jest be - cause it's June! June!

JUST SQUEEZE ME
(But Don't Tease Me)

Words by LEE GAINES
Music by DUKE ELLINGTON

Slowly, but rhythmic

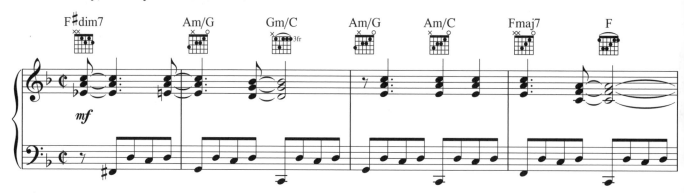

Want you to know I go for your squeez-in'.

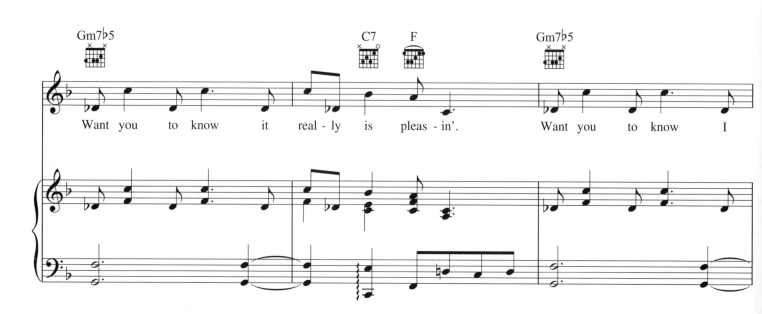

Want you to know it real-ly is pleas-in'. Want you to know I

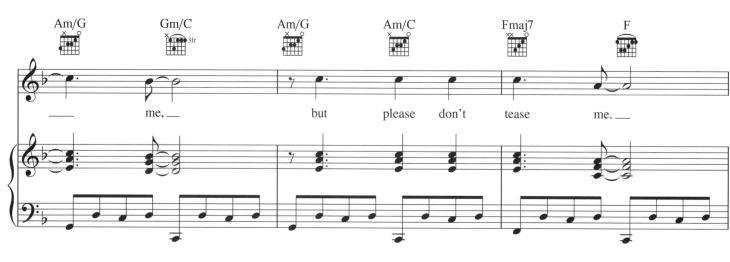

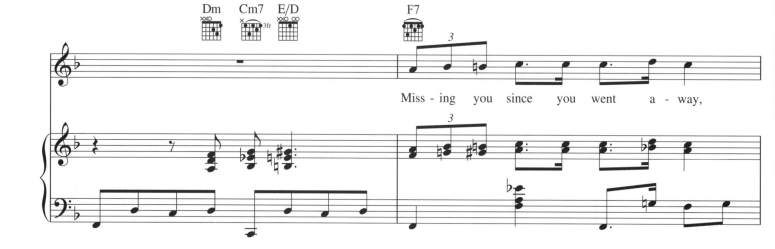

THE LAST TIME I SAW PARIS

from LADY, BE GOOD
from TILL THE CLOUDS ROLL BY

Lyrics by OSCAR HAMMERSTEIN II
Music by JEROME KERN

last time I saw Par-is her heart was warm and gay, I heard the laugh-ter of her heart in ev-'ry street ca-fé. The

LILI MARLENE

Words and Music by MACK DAVID,
HANS LEIP and NORBERT SCHULTZ

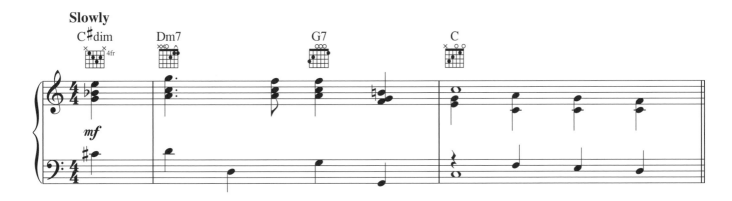

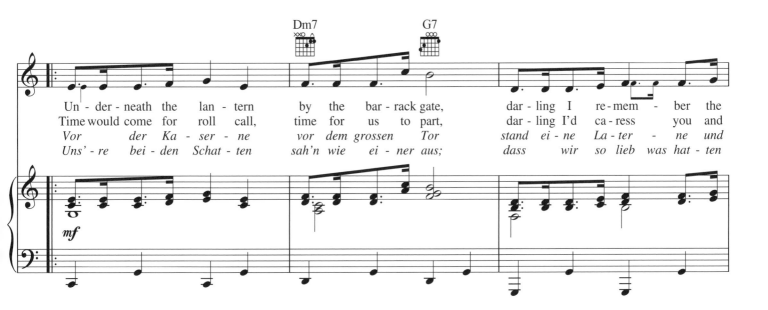

Un - der - neath the lan - tern by the bar - rack gate,
Time would come for roll call, time for us to part,
Vor der Ka - ser - ne vor dem grossen Tor
Uns' - re bei - den Schat - ten sah'n wie ei - ner aus;

dar - ling I re - mem - ber the
dar - ling I'd ca - ress you and
stand ei - ne La - ter - ne und
dass wir so lieb was hat - ten

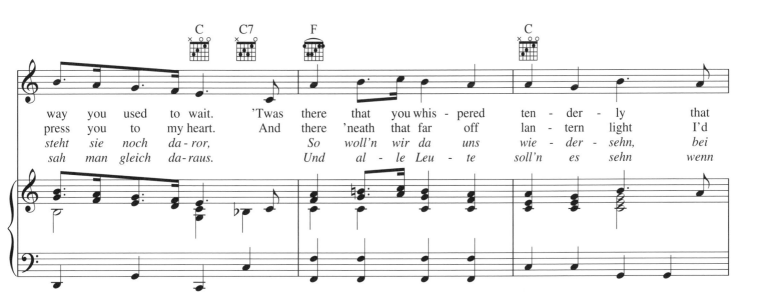

way you used to wait. 'Twas there that you whis - pered ten - der - ly that
press you to my heart. And there 'neath that far off lan - tern light I'd
steht sie noch da - ror, So woll'n wir da uns wie - der - sehn, bei
sah man gleich da - raus. Und al - le Leu - te soll'n es sehn wenn

you lov'd me, you'd al - ways be ⎫ my Li - li of the lamp - light, my
hold you tight, we'd kiss, "good - night," ⎭
der La - ter - ne woll'n wir steh'n ⎫ *wie einst Li - li Mar - leen,* *wie*
wir bei der La - ter - ne steh'n ⎭

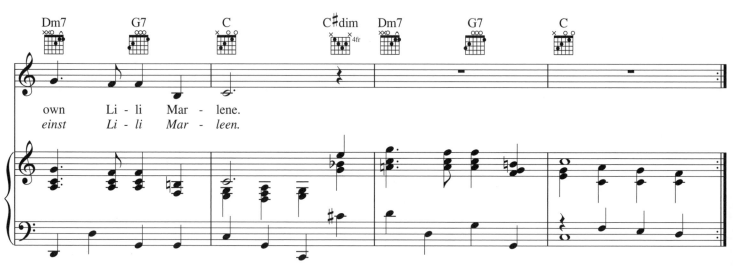

own Li - li Mar - lene.
einst Li - li Mar - leen.

Or - ders came for sail - ing some - where o - ver there, all con - fined to bar - racks was
Rest - ing in a bill - et just be - hind the line, e - ven tho' we're part - ed your
Schon rief der Po - sten: sie bla - sen Za - pfen sheich; es kann drei Ta - ge ko - sten! Ka - me
Dei - ne Schrit - te kennt sie, dei - nen zie - ren Gang, al - le A - bend brennt sie
Aus dem stil - lin Rau - me, aus der Er - de Grund hebt mich wie im Trau - me

LONG AGO
(And Far Away)
from COVER GIRL

Words by IRA GERSHWIN
Music by JEROME KERN

MANAGUA, NICARAGUA

Lyric by ALBERT GAMSE
Music by IRVING FIELDS

252

LOVE LETTERS

Theme from the Paramount Picture LOVE LETTERS

Words by EDWARD HEYMAN
Music by VICTOR YOUNG

MAÑANA

Words and Music by
PEGGY LEE and DAVE BARBOUR

Additional Lyrics

3. Oh, once I had some money but I gave it to my friend.
He said he'd pay me double, it was only for a lend.
But he said a little later that the horse she was so slow.
Why he gave the horse my money is something I don't know.

4. My brother took his suitcase and he went away to school.
My father said he only learn'd to be a silly fool.
My father said that I should learn to make a chili pot.
But then I burn'd the house down the chili was too hot.

5. The window she is broken and the rain is coming in.
If someone doesn't fix it I'll be soaking to my skin.
But if we wait a day or two the rain may go away.
And we don't need a window on such a sunny day.

MOONLIGHT IN VERMONT

Words and Music by JOHN BLACKBURN
and KARL SUESSDORF

NATURE BOY

Words and Music by
EDEN AHBEZ

OH, WHAT A BEAUTIFUL MORNIN'
from OKLAHOMA!

Lyrics by OSCAR HAMMERSTEIN II
Music by RICHARD RODGERS

Moderate Waltz

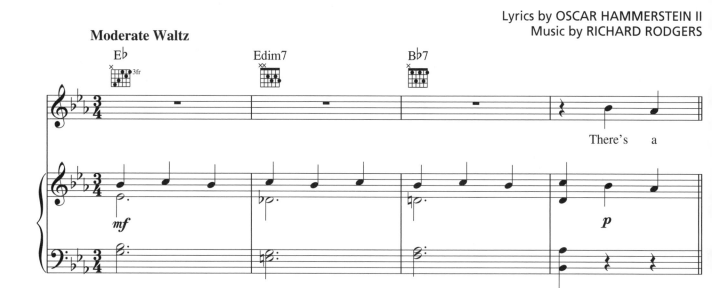

There's a

bright gold-en haze on the mead-ow, ____
cat-tle are stand-in' like stat-ues, ____
sounds of the earth are like mu-sic, ____

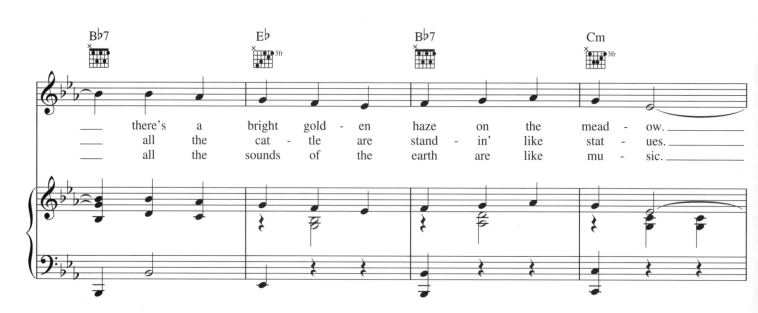

____ there's a bright gold-en haze on the mead-ow. ____
____ all the cat-tle are stand-in' like stat-ues. ____
____ all the sounds of the earth are like mu-sic. ____

OLD DEVIL MOON
from FINIAN'S RAINBOW

Words by E.Y. HARBURG
Music by BURTON LANE

THE OLD PIANO ROLL BLUES

Words and Music by
CY COBEN

Moderate Ragtime tempo

Lyrics:

I wan-na hear it a-gain, I wan-na hear it a-gain, the old pi-a-no roll blues. We're sit-tin' at an up-right, my sweet-ie and me, push-in' on the ped-als mak-in' sweet har-mo-ny. When we hear

ON A SLOW BOAT TO CHINA

By FRANK LOESSER

ONE DOZEN ROSES

Words by ROGER LEWIS and "COUNTRY" JOE WASHBURN
Music by DICK JURGENS and WALTER DONOVAN

OPEN THE DOOR, RICHARD!

Words by "DUSTY" FLETCHER and JOHN MASON
Music by JACK McVEA and DAN HOWELL

SENTIMENTAL JOURNEY

Words and Music by BUD GREEN,
LES BROWN and BEN HOMER

PISTOL PACKIN' MAMA

Words and Music by
AL DEXTER

Moderate Blues tempo

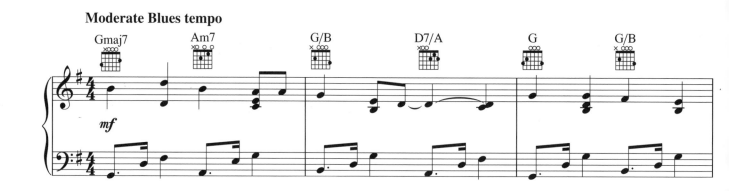

Drink - in' beer in a cab - a - ret, ___ and
She kicked out my ___ wind - shield, ___ she
Drink - in' beer in a cab - a - ret, ___ and

was I hav - in' fun! Un - til one night she
hit me o - ver the head, she cussed and cried and
danc - ing with a blonde, un - til one night she

RED ROSES FOR A BLUE LADY

Words and Music by
SID TEPPER and ROY C. BENNETT

ROUTE 66

By BOBBY TROUP

SEEMS LIKE OLD TIMES

Lyric and Music by JOHN JACOB LOEB
and CARMEN LOMBARDO

SHOO FLY PIE AND
APPLE PAN DOWDY

Lyric by SAMMY GALLOP
Music by GUY WOOD

Slow bounce

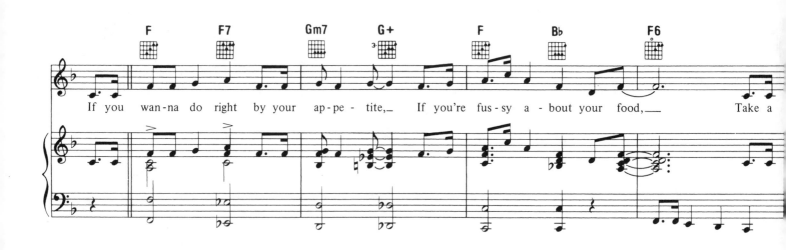

If you wan-na do right by your ap-pe-tite,__ If you're fus-sy a-bout your food,__ Take a

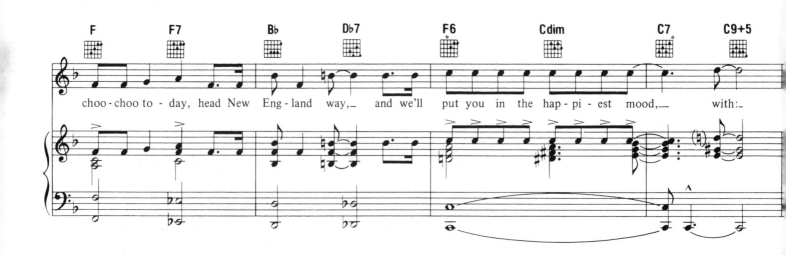

choo-choo to-day, head New Eng-land way,__ and we'll put you in the hap-pi-est mood,__ with:__

A SUNDAY KIND OF LOVE

Words and Music by BARBARA BELLE,
LOUIS PRIMA, ANITA LEONARD and STAN RHODES

SLEEPY LAGOON

Words by JACK LAWRENCE
Music by ERIC COATES

STELLA BY STARLIGHT
from the Paramount Picture THE UNINVITED

Words by NED WASHINGTON
Music by VICTOR YOUNG

THE SURREY WITH THE FRINGE ON TOP

from OKLAHOMA!

Lyrics by OSCAR HAMMERSTEIN II
Music by RICHARD RODGERS

Brightly

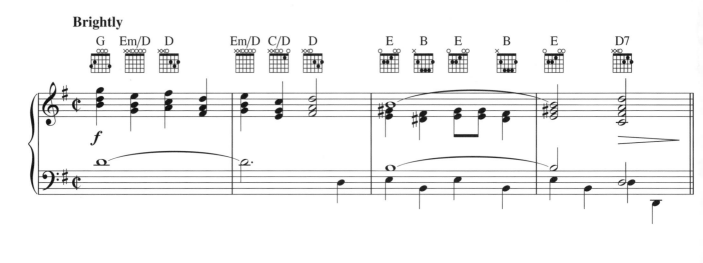

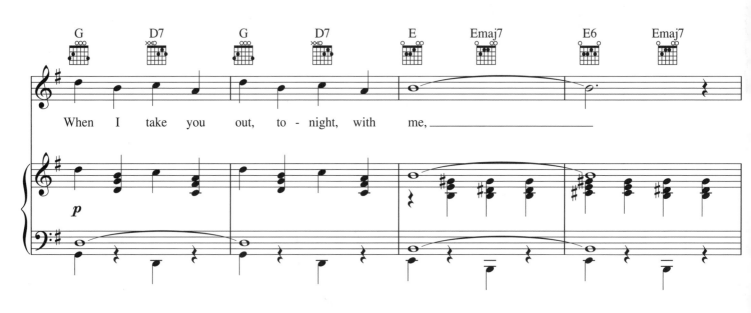

When I take you out, to-night, with me, ___

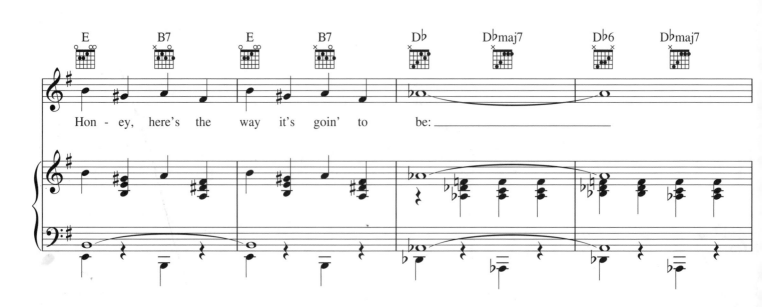

Hon-ey, here's the way it's goin' to be: ___

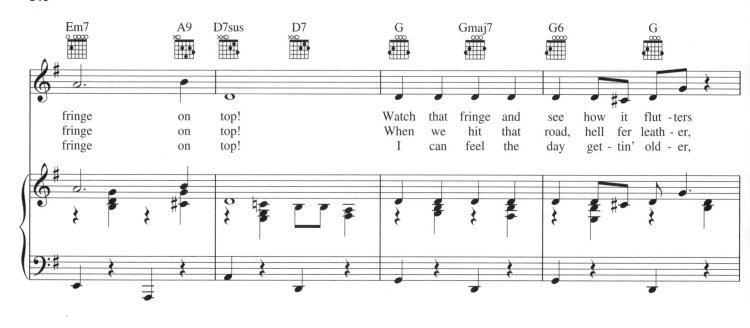

fringe on top! Watch that fringe and see how it flut -ters
fringe on top! When we hit that road, hell fer leath -er,
fringe on top! I can feel the day get -tin' old -er,

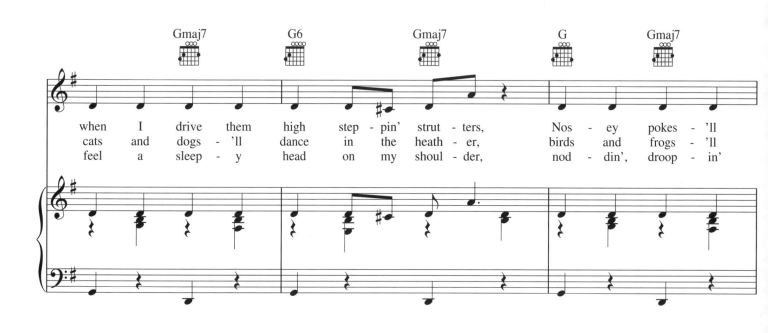

when I drive them high step -pin' strut -ters, Nos -ey pokes -'ll
cats and dogs -'ll dance in the heath -er, birds and frogs -'ll
feel a sleep -y head on my shoul -der, nod -din', droop -in'

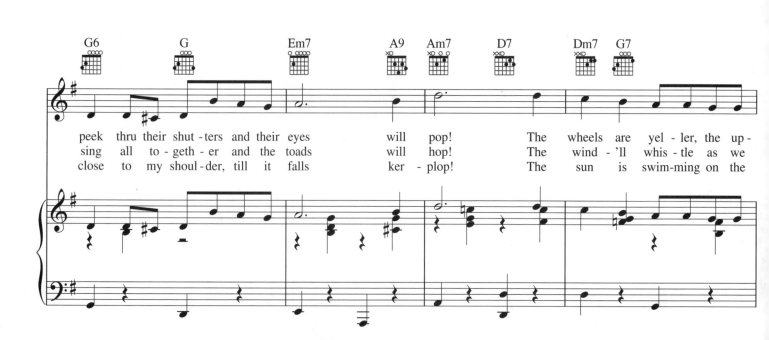

peek thru their shut -ters and their eyes will pop! The wheels are yel -ler, the up-
sing all to -geth -er and the toads will hop! The wind -'ll whis -tle as we
close to my shoul -der, till it falls ker -plop! The sun is swim -ming on the

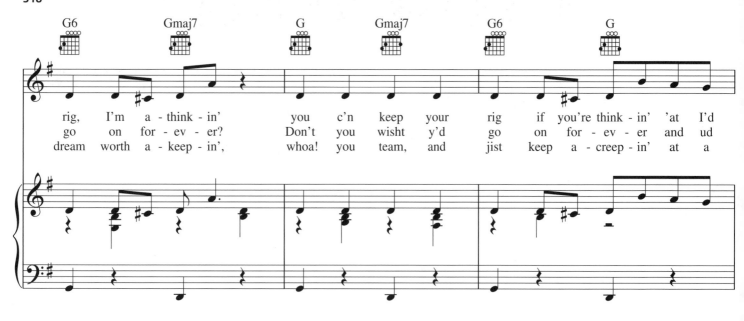

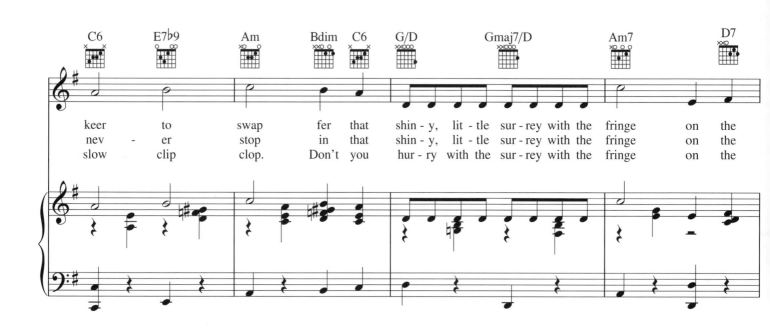

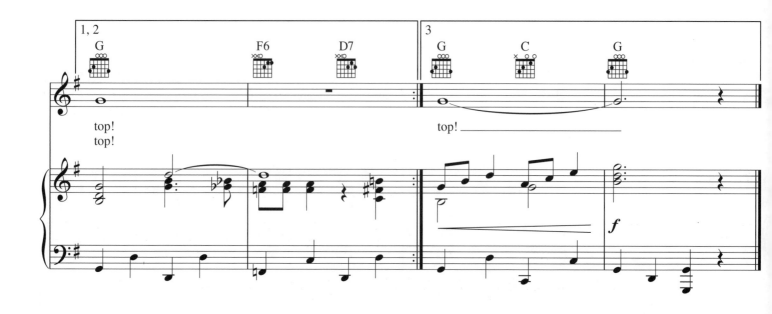

TAKE THE "A" TRAIN

Words and Music by
BILLY STRAYHORN

TANGERINE

from the Paramount Picture THE FLEET'S IN

Words by JOHNNY MERCER
Music by VICTOR SCHERTZINGER

THAT OLD BLACK MAGIC

from the Paramount Picture STAR SPANGLED RHYTHM

Words by JOHNNY MERCER
Music by HAROLD ARLEN

THERE! I'VE SAID IT AGAIN

Words and Music by
DAVE MANN and REDD EVANS

THE THINGS WE DID LAST SUMMER

Words by SAMMY CAHN
Music by JULE STYNE

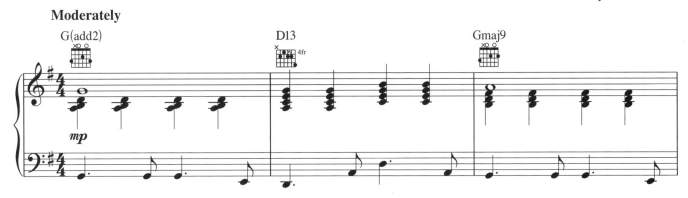

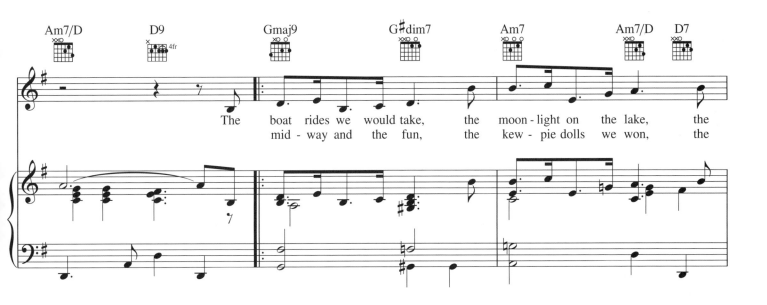

THEY SAY IT'S WONDERFUL
from the Stage Production ANNIE GET YOUR GUN

Words and Music by IRVING BERLIN

THIS NEARLY WAS MINE

from SOUTH PACIFIC

Lyrics by OSCAR HAMMERSTEIN II
Music by RICHARD RODGERS

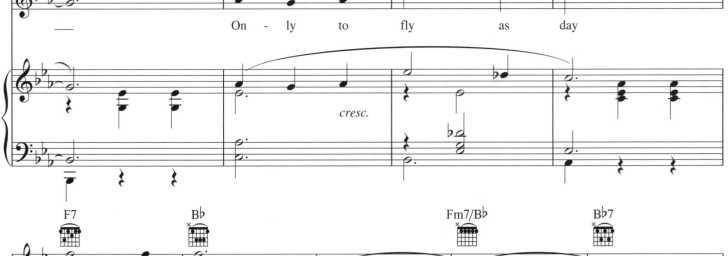

Eb   Ab   Eb7   Ab

mine. _____ Close to my heart she came _____

Eb   Bb   Eb

On - ly to fly a - way, _____

Ab   Eb7   Ab

On - ly to fly as day

cresc.

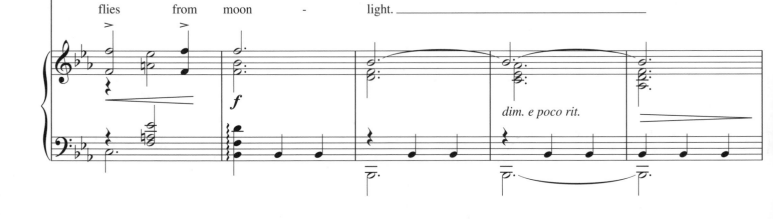

F7   Bb   Fm7/Bb   Bb7

flies from moon - light. _____

f

dim. e poco rit.

TO EACH HIS OWN

from the Paramount Picture TO EACH HIS OWN
from the Paramount Picture THE CONVERSATION

Words and Music by JAY LIVINGSTON
and RAY EVANS

WAIT TILL YOU SEE HER

from BY JUPITER

Words by LORENZ HART
Music by RICHARD RODGERS

WHEN MY BLUE MOON TURNS TO GOLD AGAIN

Words and Music by WILEY WALKER
and GENE SULLIVAN

With movement

(There'll Be Bluebirds Over)
THE WHITE CLIFFS OF DOVER

Words by NAT BURTON
Music by WALTER KENT

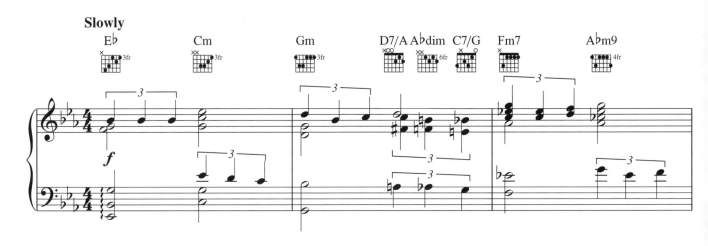

I'll nev-er for-get the peo-ple I met
When night shad-ows fall I al-ways re-call

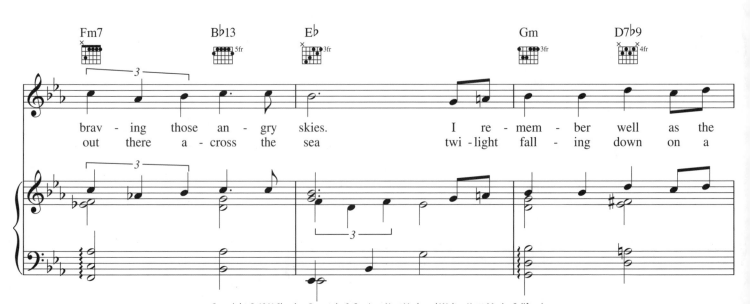

brav-ing those an-gry skies.
out there a-cross the sea

I re-mem-ber well as the
twi-light fall-ing down on a

WHY DON'T YOU DO RIGHT
(Get Me Some Money, Too!)

By JOE McCOY

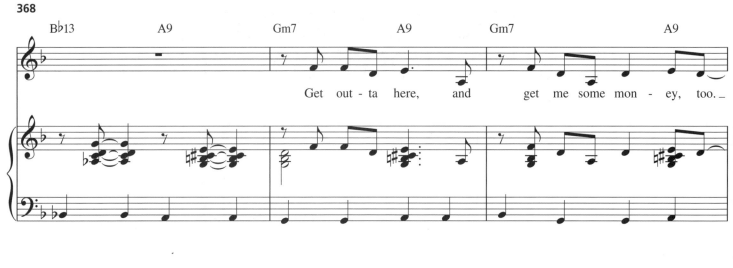

Get out-ta here, and get me some mon-ey, too.

Why don't you do right

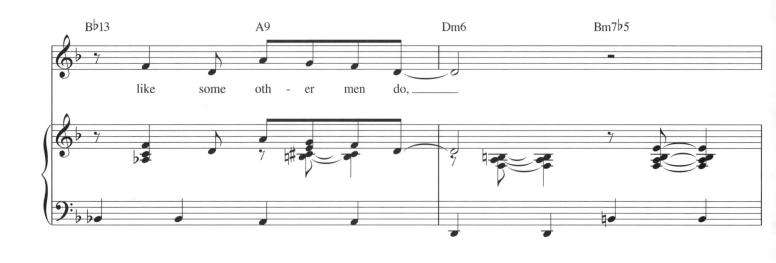

like some oth - er men do,

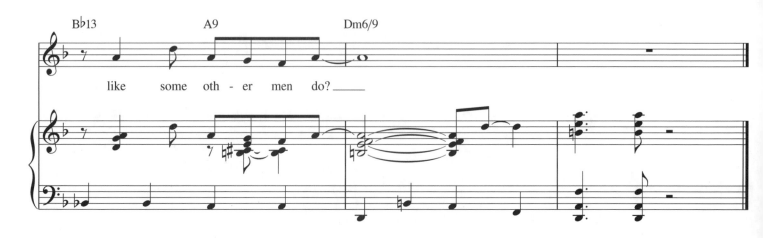

like some oth - er men do?

YOU'RE NOBODY 'TIL SOMEBODY LOVES YOU

Words and Music by RUSS MORGAN,
LARRY STOCK and JAMES CAVANAUGH

YES INDEED

Words and Music by SY OLIVER

With a Slow, measured beat

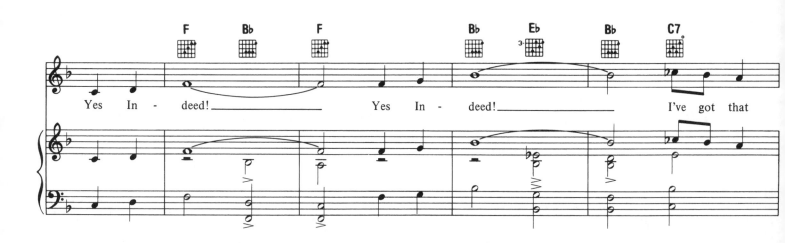

Yes In - deed! _____ Yes In - deed! _____ I've got that

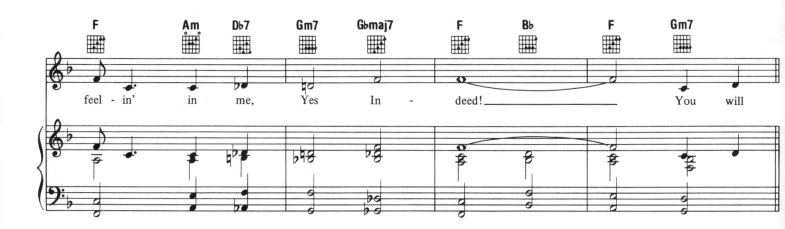

feel - in' in me, Yes In - deed! _____ You will

YOU BELONG TO MY HEART
(Solamente Una Vez)

Music and Spanish words by AGUSTIN LARA
English Words by RAY GILBERT

You be-long to my heart ___ now and for-ev-er, ___ and our love had its start ___ not long a-go. ___

So-la-men-te u-na vez ___ a-mé en la vi-da, ___ so-la-men-te u-na vez y na-da más. ___

YOU DON'T KNOW WHAT LOVE IS

Words and Music by DON RAYE
and GENE DePAUL

YOU'D BE SO NICE TO COME HOME TO

from SOMETHING TO SHOUT ABOUT

Words and Music by
COLE PORTER

Moderately slow, with feeling

It's not that you're fair-er, than a lot of girls just as pleas-in', that I doff my hat as a wor-ship-per at your shrine. ___ It's

ZIP-A-DEE-DOO-DAH

from Walt Disney's SONG OF THE SOUTH

Words by RAY GILBERT
Music by ALLIE WRUBEL

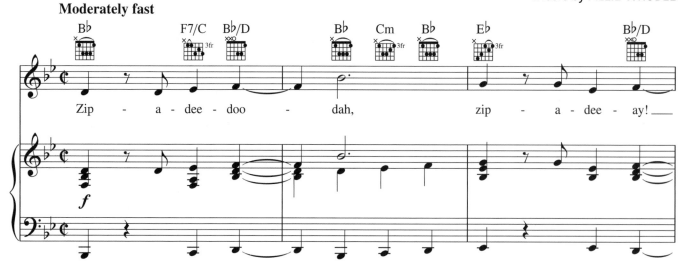

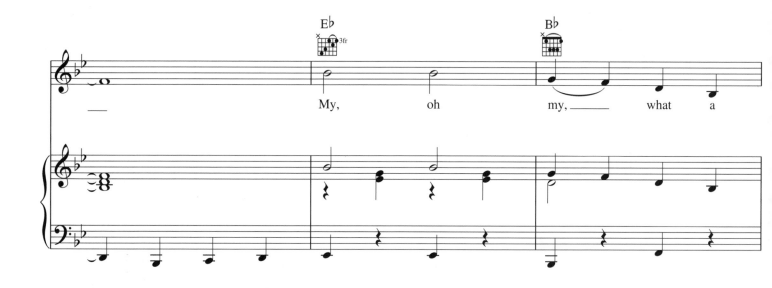

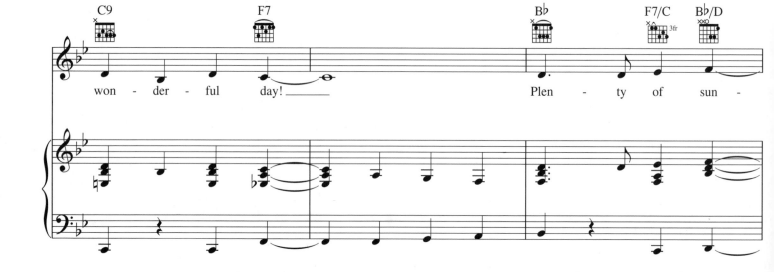

HAL·LEONARD ESSENTIAL SONGS

Play the best songs from the Roaring '20s to today! Each collection features up to 100 of the most memorable songs of each decade, arranged in Piano/Vocal/Guitar format or in our world-famous, patented E-Z Play® Today notation. Each book also includes info about the composers or from the Billboard charts: the songs' peak position and the year they charted.

ESSENTIAL SONGS – THE 1920s

Over 100 songs that shaped the decade, including: Ain't We Got Fun? • All by Myself • April Showers • Basin Street Blues • Bill • The Birth of the Blues • Blue Skies • Bye Bye Blackbird • California, Here I Come • Can't Help Lovin' Dat Man • Chicago (That Toddlin' Town) • Five Foot Two, Eyes of Blue (Has Anybody Seen My Girl?) • I Can't Give You Anything but Love • I Wanna Be Loved by You • I'm Looking Over a Four Leaf Clover • If You Knew Susie (Like I Know Susie) • Indian Love Call • Let a Smile Be Your Umbrella • Look for the Silver Lining • Makin' Whoopee! • Manhattan • Moonlight and Roses (Bring Mem'ries of You) • My Blue Heaven • Ol' Man River • Puttin' On the Ritz • St. Louis Blues • Second Hand Rose • Stardust • Thou Swell • Toot, Toot, Tootsie! (Good-bye!) • 'Way down Yonder in New Orleans • Who's Sorry Now • Yes Sir, That's My Baby • and more.
00311200 Piano/Vocal/Guitar.................................$24.95
00100214 E-Z Play Today #23...............................$19.94

ESSENTIAL SONGS – THE 1930s

Over 100 essential songs from the 1930s, including: All the Things You Are • April in Paris • Autumn in New York • Body and Soul • Cheek to Cheek • Cherokee (Indian Love Song) • Easy to Love (You'd Be So Easy to Love) • Falling in Love with Love • Georgia on My Mind • Heart and Soul • How Deep Is the Ocean (How High Is the Sky) • I'll Be Seeing You • I've Got My Love to Keep Me Warm • In a Sentimental Mood • In the Mood • Isn't It Romantic? • The Lady Is a Tramp • Mood Indigo • My Funny Valentine • Pennies from Heaven • September Song • You Are My Sunshine • and more.
00311193 Piano/Vocal/Guitar $24.95
00100206 E-Z Play Today #24 ....$19.95

ESSENTIAL SONGS – THE 1940s

An amazing collection of over 100 songs that came out of the 1940s, including: Ac-cent-tchu-ate the Positive • Anniversary Song • Be Careful, It's My Heart • Bewitched • Boogie Woogie Bugle Boy • Don't Get Around Much Anymore • Have I Told You Lately That I Love You • I'll Remember April • Is You Is, or Is You Ain't (Ma' Baby) • It Could Happen to You • Might As Well Be Spring • Route 66 • Sentimental Journey • Stella by Starlight • The Surrey with the Fringe on Top • Take the "A" Train • They Say It's Wonderful • This Nearly Was Mine • You'd Be So Nice to Come Home To • You're Nobody 'til Somebody Loves You • and more.
00311192 P/V/G $24.95
00100207 E-Z Play Today #25 ....$19.95

ESSENTIAL SONGS – THE 1950s

Over 100 pivotal songs from the 1950s, including: All Shook Up • At the Hop • Blueberry Hill • Bye Bye Love • Chantilly Lace • Don't Be Cruel (To a Heart That's True) • Fever • Great Balls of Fire • High Hopes • Kansas City • Love and Marriage • Mister Sandman • Mona Lisa • (You've Got) Personality • Rock Around the Clock • Sea of Love • Sixteen Tons • Smoke Gets in Your Eyes • Tennessee Waltz • Tom Dooley • Twilight Time • Wear My Ring Around Your Neck • Wonderful! Wonderful! • and more.
00311191 Piano/Vocal/Guitar $24.95
00100208 E-Z Play Today #51 ....$19.95

ESSENTIAL SONGS – THE 1960s

Over 100 '60s essentials, including: Baby Love • Barbara Ann • Born to Be Wild • California Girls • Can't Buy Me Love • Dancing in the Street • Downtown • Good Vibrations • Hang on Sloopy • Hey Jude • I Heard It Through the Grapevine • It's Not Unusual • My Guy • Respect • Something Spooky • Stand by Me • Stop! in the Name of Love • Suspicious Minds • A Time for Us (Love Theme) • Twist and Shout • Will You Love Me Tomorrow (Will You Still Love Me Tomorrow) • Yesterday • You Keep Me Hangin' On • and more.
00311190 Piano/Vocal/Guitar $24.95
00100209 E-Z Play Today #52 ....$19.95

ESSENTIAL SONGS – THE 1970s

A fantastic collection of over 80 of the best songs from the '70s, including: ABC • Afternoon Delight • American Pie • American Woman • At Seventeen • Baker Street • Band on the Run • Bohemian Rhapsody • The Boys Are Back in Town • Come Sail Away • Da Ya Think I'm Sexy • Do You Know Where You're Going To? • Dust in the Wind • Feelings (¿Dime?) • Hot Child in the City • I Feel the Earth Move • I'll Be There • Knock Three Times • Let It Be • Morning Has Broken • Smoke on the Water • Take a Chance on Me • The Way We Were • What's Going On • You Are the Sunshine of My Life • You Light Up My Life • You're So Vain • Your Song • and more.
00311189 Piano/Vocal/Guitar $24.95
00100210 E-Z Play Today #53 ....$19.95

FOR MORE INFORMATION, SEE YOUR LOCAL MUSIC DEALER, OR WRITE TO:

HAL·LEONARD® CORPORATION
7777 W. BLUEMOUND RD. P.O. BOX 13819 MILWAUKEE, WI 53213

ESSENTIAL SONGS – THE 1980s

Over 70 classics from the age of new wave, power pop, and hair metal, including: Abracadabra • Against All Odds (Take a Look at Me Now) • Axel F • Call Me • Centerfold • Could I Have This Dance • Didn't We Almost Have It All • Don't You (Forget About Me) • Ebony and Ivory • Footloose • The Heat Is On • Higher Love • Hurts So Good • Jump • Love Shack • Man in the Mirror • Manic Monday • Material Girl • Rosanna • The Safety Dance • Sister Christian • Somewhere Out There • Take My Breath Away (Love Theme) • Time After Time • Up Where We Belong • We Are the World • What's Love Got to Do with It • and more.
00311188 Piano/Vocal/Guitar $24.95
00100210 E-Z Play Today #54..............................$19.95

ESSENTIAL SONGS – THE 1990s

68 essential songs from the 1990s featuring country-crossover, swing revival, the birth of grunge, and much more! Songs include: All 4 Love • Blaze of Glory • Blue • Can You Feel the Love Tonight • Change the World • Come to My Window • (Everything I Do) I Do It for You • Fields of Gold • From a Distance • I Finally Found Someone • I Will Remember You • Ironic • Janie's Got a Gun • Livin' La Vida Loca • More Than Words • Semi-Charmed Life • Smells like Teen Spirit • This Kiss • Two Princes • Under the Bridge • Walking in Memphis • Zoot Suit Riot • and more.
00311187 Piano/Vocal/Guitar $24.95

ESSENTIAL SONGS – THE 2000s

58 of the best songs that brought in the new millennium, including: Accidentally in Love • Always • Beautiful • Breathe • Calling All Angels • Clocks • Complicated • Don't Know Why • Get the Party Started • Give Me Just One Night (Una Noche) • Hey Ya! • I Hope You Dance • Jenny from the Block • 1985 • Out of My Heart (Into Your Head) • She Bangs • So Yesterday • Somewhere Out There • The Space Between • Thank You • There You'll Be • This Love • A Thousand Miles • Underneath Your Clothes • Wherever You Will Go • Who Let the Dogs Out • You Raise Me Up • and more.
00311186 Piano/Vocal/Guitar $24.95

Complete contents listings are available online at **www.halleonard.com**

Prices, contents and availability subject to change without notice.